THE HILL OF VISION

MACMILLAN AND CO., Limited
LONDON · BOMBAY · CALCUTTA · MADRAS
MELBOURNE

THE MACMILLAN COMPANY
NEW YORK · BOSTON · CHICAGO
DALLAS · SAN FRANCISCO

THE MACMILLAN CO. OF CANADA, Ltd.
TORONTO

THE
HILL OF VISION

BY

JAMES STEPHENS

AUTHOR OF "INSURRECTIONS"

MACMILLAN AND CO., LIMITED
ST. MARTIN'S STREET, LONDON
1925

PRINTED IN GREAT BRITAIN

TO

MY WIFE

CONTENTS

Everything that I can spy
Through the circle of my eye,
Everything that I can see
Has been woven out of me.
I have sown the stars; I threw
Clouds of morn and noon and eve
In the deeps and steeps of blue;
And each thing that I perceive,
Sun and sea and mountain high,
Are made and moulded by my eye:
Closing it, I do but find
Darkness, and a little wind.

A PRELUDE AND A SONG

THE PRELUDE

(1)

Song! glad indeed I am that we have met,
Too long, my sister, you have stayed
    from me ;
Almost I fancied that you could forget
Those binding promises, that you would be
Under the slender interlacing boughs
Waiting for me.

I came and looked about on every side
But where you hid away I could not see ;
And first I searched among the meadows
    wide,
And up the hill, and under every tree,
And down the stream to see if you were
    there
Waiting for me.

3

But when I did not find you in the mead,
Or by the stream, or under any tree,
I thought you had forgotten we agreed,
Not long ago, that surely you would be
Under the slender interlacing boughs
Waiting for me.

You came to me I do not know from where:
I stood and saw you not, I turn and see:
Have you sprung to me from the sunny
*   air?*
Or in the long grass did you curiously
Watch while I wandered, laughing as
*   you lay*
Waiting for me?

And you have brought your pipe! let
*   us begin,*
Against your skill I match my poetry:
A kiss if I should fail, and if I win
A kiss the same—tune not your melody
Too high at first, I shall not keep you long
Waiting for me.

(2)

O wind that through the winding,
   green-grown ways,
At morn or eve doth tender-piping
   go ;
Or from the crag, with trumpetings of
   praise,
Doth fright the lambs that crop the
   mead below ;
From cave or hill or wood
Or bustling cloud come thou in merry
   mood ;
Leave those wild murmurings that
   make to weep,
Your long-blown pealing trumpet put
   away,
And where a merry holiday we keep
In sunny fields come thou and dance
   and leap
And sing for joy with us the live-long
   day.

Oft we have seen you linger in the
     corn,
And all the red caps nodding at your
     play;
Or in the croft on breezy summer morn
Blowing the light-oared thistle balls
     away :
And one day, unobserved, we watched
     you where
You stole a ribbon from a maiden
     slim,
And blew it to a boy who stood and
     prayed,
Which, e'er he kissed, you snatched
     away from him,
And whirled it back again unto the
     maid
Who was his only hope and thought
     and care ;
And while he sighed and while she
     laughed you took
The ribbon up and soused it in a brook,
Lost to the lips of lover anywhere.

And yet again we saw
You playing with the milkmaids in
    the shaw,
Where, standing near, a satyr trained
    his eye
If there was aught forbidden he might
    see,
And crept upon you with a mind to
    spy
The cause of that uproarious jollity :
Then, when the wild one looked too
    curiously,
You blew his own rough beard and
    shaggy hair,
And blinded him who stared so
    greedily,
Because it was not right that he should
    see
The milkmaid's kirtle that you meddled
    there.

So you can laugh and play ;
Come pipe with us and join our holiday :

Join in our song and you may chance
    to win
For you are free of thought, and hath
    no care
To question, did the sinner, told of, sin ?
Or, who has seen ? or, why, or when,
    or where ?
No longer bide
By screaming crag or murmurous
    waterside,
But your quaint careless lute bring
    with you here
And sing to us and we shall sing to
    you,
Until we find who has the finest ear,
And who the sweetest voice and gayest
    cheer,
And give to him the praise that is his
    due.

(3)

O nymphs ! if ye will come from spring
or lake,
Or where the sedge is wavering in the
stream,
To dance with us and with us to
partake
A careless fellowship, or with us dream
Stretched idly on the grass to watch
the gleam
Of sunlight through the leaves—we
welcome true
And will applaud your shy romantic
theme,
Your delicate wild tales and music
new ;
And fair respectful courtesy extend to
you.

But ye, goat-footed fellows, keep away,
Nor through the bushes strain your
wily eyes,

For ye would love to spoil our holiday,
And fright the nymphs away with
sudden cries,
And whispers lewd, and vicious enter-
prise :
—But if ye promise truly to be good,
Then come with clamant reeds and
improvise,
With antic dance and savour of the
wood
And all the games ye learned in sunlit
solitude.

(4)

Round the trees ye danced and flew
While the boughs danced down to
  see,
And the sun was dancing through
Leafy spaces on the tree :
The daisies danced, the meadow-sweet,
All the swaying grassy blades
Danced behind the dancing feet
Of the merry dancing maids.

Left and right and swing around,
Soar and dip and fall for glee,
Happy sky and bird and ground,
Happy wind and happy tree :
Happy minions, dancing mad,
Joy is guide enough for you,
Cure the world of good and bad,
And teach us innocence anew.

Good and bad and right and wrong,
Wave the silly words away :
This is wisdom to be strong,
This is virtue to be gay :
Let us sing and dance until
We shall know the final art,
How to banish good and ill
With the laughter of the heart.

THE SONG

(1)

I HAVE a black, black mind !
What shall I do ?
If I could fly and leave it all behind,
Scaling the blue,
Over the trees and up and out of sight,
And wrong and right
Naming them for the nonsense that
    they are !
I'd leave them far,
Drop them behind with this and that
    and these,
The tyrannies
That promised to be blessings and are
    woes ;
The crows
I fancied to be singing birds,

The words
That drowse and buzz and drone and
  never stay.
Oh ! far away !
Over the pine trees and the mountain
  top,
Never to stop
Lifting wide wings, to fly and fly and
  fly
Into the sky.

(2)

If I had wings just like a bird
I would not say a single word,
I'd spread my wings and fly away
Beyond the reach of yesterday.

If I could swim just like a fish
I'd give my little tail a swish,
I'd swim ten days and nights and then
I never would be found again.

Or if I were a comet bright
I'd drop in secret every night
Ten million miles, and no one would
Know where I kept my solitude.

But I am not a bird or fish
Or comet, so I need not wish,
And need not try to get away
Beyond the reach of yesterday.

(3)

No more of woeful Misery I sing !
Let her go moping down the pavéd way ;
While to the sunny fields, and every-
    thing
That laughs, and to the birds that sing,
I pass along and tune my happy lay :
O sunny sky !
O meadows that the happy clouds are
    drifting by !

I go at ease by the easy-sliding stream
As by a friend : I dance in solitude
Among the trees ; I lie and gaze and
    dream
Along the grass, or hearken to the
    theme
A lark discourses to her tender brood :
O sunny sky !
O meadows that the happy clouds are
    drifting by !

There is a thrush lives snugly in a wall,
She lets me come and peep into her nest,
She lets me see and touch the speckled
    ball
Under her wing, and does not fear at
    all,
Although her shy companion is dis-
    tressed :
O sunny sky !
O meadows that the happy clouds are
    drifting by !

Sing out, sing out again ye birds of
    joy !
Tell yet from branch and bough your
    endless tale
Of happiness that nothing can annoy ;
Altho' your mates seem timorous and
    coy
If ye sing high enough how can ye fail ?
O sunny sky !
O meadows that the happy clouds are
    drifting by !

On every side, far as the eye can see,
The round horizon, like a bosom's
    swell,
Seems brooding in a sweet maternity,
Where no thing may be hurt, not
    even me,
But she will stoop and kiss and make
    us well :
O sunny sky !
O meadows that the happy clouds are
    drifting by !

I am the brother of each bird and tree
And everything that grows—your chil-
    dren glad ;
Their hearts are in my heart, their
    ecstasy :
O Mother of all mothers, comfort me,
Give me your breast for I am very
    sad :
O sunny sky !
O meadows that the happy clouds are
    drifting by !

(4)

I wandered far away in lucid morn,
When summer did the happy trees
    adorn ;
I left all that I knew of discontent,
Of sorrow and distress and angry
    pain,
And did not say to any where I
    went,
Or when, or if I would return again
From leafy solitude.

I wandered far away and far away,
And was as happy as a person may
To hear the birds in wild wood sing
    their strain,
Each hid in bough, a young and
    joyous band,
Who had no care save only to attain
The food and shelter that lay every
    hand
In leafy solitude.

I wandered far away and did not turn :
At such a song my heart began to burn,
And joy that I had never known before,
And tears that had no meaning I
    could say,
Came from the music that the birds
    did pour
To me as I went softly on my way
In leafy solitude.

I wandered far away and I was glad :
I knew the rapture that the forest had :
And every bird was good to me and
    said
A kindly word e'er I had passed him by,
The cheery squirrel sat and ate his
    bread
And did not fear me when I ventured
    nigh
His leafy solitude.

(5)

O birds, my brothers, sing to me once
    more
E'er I return again to whence I came,
Give me your joy, your innocence,
    your lore,
Your air-born, wind-blown ecstasy I
    claim
Because ye truly are my brothers dear :
Sing to me once again before I go from
    here.

In woodland ways again we may not
    meet ;
Under the slender interlacing boughs,
Where all day long the sunbeams flash
    and fleet
On leaf and grass and wing,
And all day long ye sing
And hold carouse :
Because ye truly are my brothers dear
Sing to me once again before I go from
    here.

All things must cease at last ;
Night cometh after day
And day is past.
All things must end,
And friend from loving friend
At the long last will rise and go away ;
And from the slender interlacing boughs
The leaves that flutter now must fail
    and fall ;
The time is come I may no more
    carouse,
Farewell to ye and good-bye to ye all :
Because ye truly are my brothers dear
Sing to me once again before I go from
    here.

(6)

O cloud aloof, afar, scarce to be seen !
O unattainable ! to you alone
I lift my wings,
To you I lean,
I yearn to you beyond all other things ;
Desperate I am for you, for you I
    moan ;
I struggle to you and I always fail,
I sink and fall, I fall for ever down,
Deep down where you are not, with-
    out avail
Or help or hope : a clod am I, a
    clown
Whose wry mouth laughs in fury at
    his thought ;
A discontent without a word to say ;
A hope that cannot fasten upon aught ;
A nothing that is anything it may ;
A moodiness, a hatred and a love
Mixed through of good and bad that
    cannot show ;

But you are calm at morning as a dove
That broods in nest is calm, and in
    the glow
Of day you meet joy everywhere with
    joy,
And, as a woman looking on the child
That sleeps upon her arm has no annoy,
With brow of that content and breast
    as mild,
You rest upon the evening and its
    gold,
Its rose and pearl, its tender green and
    grey :
O peacefulness that never can be
    told !
O far away !
Over the pine trees and the mountain
    top,
Never to stop
Lifting wide wings, to fly and fly and fly
Into the sky.

(7)

Weary indeed I know that this world
    is ;
Then do not sing to me a song of woe,
But tune your pipe to all of aery bliss
Ye can remember, and I will not miss
To join in every chorus that I know :
Give me the very rapture of your song
Else I may go away with thoughts that
    do ye wrong.

Sing sweetly, sweetly, once again to me,
Sing me the joy ye have not reached
    to yet ;
E'er I go hence give me your ecstasy,
E'er I go hence, e'er far away I flee
Give me the joy which I may not
    forget :
The very inner rapture of your song :
Else I may go away with thoughts that
    do ye wrong.

(8)

The joyful song that welcomes in the
    spring,
The tender mating song so bravely shy,
The song that builds the nest, the
    merry ring
When the long wait is ended and ye
    bring
The young birds out and teach them
    how to fly.

Sing to me of the beech-nuts on the
    ground,
And of the first wild flight at early
    dawn,
And of the store of berries some one
    found
And hid away, until ye gathered round
And ate them while he shrieked upon
    the lawn.

Sing of the swinging nest upon the tree,
And of your mates who call and hide
    away,
And of the sun that shines exceedingly,
And of the leaves that dance, and all
    the glee
And rapture that begins at break of
    day.

(9)

Follow, follow, follow !
Blackbird, thrush and swallow ;
The air is soft, the sun is dancing through
The dancing boughs ;
A little while me company along
And I will go with you :
Arouse, arouse !
Among the leaves I sing my pleasant
    song.

Blackbird, thrush and swallow !
Indeed the visits that I pay are few,
Then come to me as I have come to you :
O follow, follow, follow !
Leave for a little time your nested
    boughs
And me accompany along,
Join me while I am happy :
Rouse, O rouse !
Among the leaves I sing my pleasant
    song.

Sky, sky,
On high,
O gentle majesty !
Come all ye happy birds and follow,
    follow
Under the slender interlacing boughs
Blackbird, thrush and swallow !
No longer in the sunlight sit and drowse
But me accompany along ;
No longer be ye mute :
Arouse, arouse !
Among the leaves I sing my pleasant
    song.

Lift, lift, ye happy birds,
Lift song and wing,
And sing and fly,
And fly again and sing
Up to the very blueness of the sky
Your happy words :
O follow, follow, follow !
Where I go racing through the shady
    ways,

Blackbird, thrush and swallow,
Shouting aloud our ecstasy of praise :
Under the slender interlacing boughs
Me company along,
The sun is coming with us :
Rouse, O rouse !
Among the leaves I sing my pleasant
    song.

(10)

Reach up my wings !
Now broaden into space and carry me
Beyond where any lark that sings
Can get :
Into the utmost sharp tenuity,
The breathing - point, the start, the
    scarcely-stirred
High slenderness which never any bird
Has winged to yet !
The moon peace and the star peace
    and the peace
Of chilly sunlight :
To the void of space,
The emptiness, the giant curve, the
    great
Wide-stretching arms wherein the gods
    embrace
And stars are born and suns :
Where germinate
All fruitful seed, where life and death
    are one,

Where all things that are not their
 times await ;
Where all things that have been again
 are gone :
Deep Womb of Promise ! back to thee
 again
And forth, revivified, all things
Do come and go,
Do wax and wane into and from thy
 garden ;
There the flower springs,
Therein does grow
The bud of hope, the miracle to come
For whose dear advent we are striving
 dumb and joyless :
Garden of Delight
That God has sowed !
In thee the flower of flowers,
The apple of our tree,
The banner on our towers,
The recompense, the end of misery,
The mightiness, the purity, the light
Whom we are working to has his abode :

Until our back and forth, our life and
    death
And life again, our going and return
Prepare the way : until with latest
    breath,
Deep-drawn and agonized, for him we
    burn
A path : for him prepare
Laughter and love and singing every-
    where,
A morning and a sunrise and a day !
O, far away !
Over the pine trees and the mountain
    top
Never to stop
Lifting wide wings, I fly and fly and fly
Into the sky.

(11)

*Song ! I am tired to death ! here let me
    lie
Where we have paced the moving trees
    along,
Till I recover from my ecstasy :
Farewell my Song.*

*Once more unto your pipe I lend my
    rhyme
Who paced in woodland ways with you
    along ;
We have been happy for a little time :
Farewell my Song.*

*Soon, soon return or all my world is
    naught ;
Come back and we shall pace the woods
    along,
And tell unto each other all our thought :
Farewell my Song.*

And when again you do come back to me
Under the sounding trees we'll pace along,
While to your pipe I raise my poetry :
Farewell my Song.

IN THE POPPY FIELD

MAD Patsy said, he said to me,
That every morning he could see
An angel walking on the sky ;
Across the sunny skies of morn
He threw great handfuls far and nigh
Of poppy seed among the corn ;
And then, he said, the angels run
To see the poppies in the sun.

'A poppy is a devil weed,'
I said to him—he disagreed :
He said the devil had no hand
In spreading flowers tall and fair
Through corn and rye and meadow land,
And gurth and barrow everywhere :
The devil has not any flower,
But only money in his power.

36

And then he stretched out in the sun
And rolled upon his back for fun :
He kicked his legs and roared for joy
Because the sun was shining down,
He said he was a little boy
And wouldn't work for any clown :
He ran and laughed behind a bee,
And danced for very ecstasy.

THE FULNESS OF TIME

On a rusty iron throne
Past the furthest star of space
I saw Satan sit alone,
Old and haggard was his face ;
For his work was done, and he
Rested in eternity.

And to him from out the sun
Came his father and his friend
Saying, " Now the work is done
Enmity is at an end " :
And he guided Satan to
Paradises that he knew.

Gabriel without a frown,
Uriel without a spear,

Raphael came singing down,
Welcoming their ancient peer;
And they seated him beside
One who had been crucified.

LIGHT-O'-LOVE

AND now, at last, I must away,
But if I tend another fire
In some man's house this you will say
—It is not that her love doth tire :
This is the price she has to pay,
For bread she gets no other way,
Still dreaming of her heart's desire.

And so she went out from the door
While I sat quiet in my chair :
She ran back once, again—no more ;
I heard a footstep on the stair,
A lifted latch ; one moment fleet
I heard the noises of the street,
Then silence booming everywhere.

NUCLEOLUS

I LOOKED from Mount Derision at
Two ivory thrones that were in space,
Whereon a man and woman sat,
The very parallels of grace,
Not lovelier has ever been
By mortal seen.

Then one unto the other said,
—Tell me the secret, hidden well,
Which you have never utteréd,
And I to you again will tell
My guarded thought, and we shall know
Each other so—

Then he—When those who pray beside
My holy altars do not bear
A gift I turn my face aside

And do not listen to the prayer,
But whoso brings a gift shall see
The proof of me—-

And she—When, on a festal day,
Youth kneels by youth before my
    shrine
I think, if he or he might lay
A ruddy cheek to mine
And comfort my sick soul, I'd lay
My crown away—

THE SOOTHERER

O LITTLE JOY, why do you run so fast
Waving behind you as you go away
Your tiny hand ?   You smiled at me
    and cast
A silver apple, asking me to play :
But when I ran to pick the apple up
You ran the other way.

Little One !   White One !   Shy Little
    Gay Sprite !
Do not turn your head across your
    shoulder
To mock at me ; it is not right
That you should laugh at me, for I
    am older :
Throw me the silver apple once again
You little scolder.

I love you very dearly, yes I do ;
I never saw a girl like you before
In any place. You are more sweetly
    new
Than a May moon : you are my store,
My secret and my treasure and the pulse
Of my heart's core.

Throw me the silver apple—I will run
And pick it up and give it you again :
Dear Heart ! Sweet Laugher !—throw
    it then for fun
And not for me—if you will but remain !
. . . Nay do not run ; I'll stand thus
    far away
And not complain.

Never before—or only one or two :
I did not like them nearly half so well,
Nor half of half so well as I like you,
Throw me the silver apple and I'll tell
Their names, and what I used to say
    to them,
—The first was Nell.

Throw me the apple and I'll tell you
    more ;
—She had a lovely face, but she was
    fat :
We clung together when the rain
    would pour
Under a tree or hedge, and often sat
Through long, still, sunny hours—Tell
    what she said ?
I'll not do that.

I really couldn't, no, it would be wrong
And utterly unfair, I will not say a word
Of any girl—your voice is like the song
I heard this morning from a soaring bird
. . . I'll whisper then if you come
    close to me,
—You've hardly stirred !

She said she loved me better than her
    life.
—You need not laugh, she said so
    anyway,

And meant it too, and longed to be
    my wife :
She kissed me many times and wept
    to stay
Within my arms, and did not ever want
To go away.

But she was fat, I will admit that's true:
And so I hid when she came seeking me.
If she had been as beautiful as you . . . !
You are as slender as a growing tree,
And when you move the blood goes
    leaping through
The heart of me.

The other girl ?   Yes, she is very fair :
Her feet are lighter than the clouds on
    high,
And there is morn and noonday in her
    hair,
And mellow, sunny evenings in her eye,
And all day long she sings just like a lark
Up in the sky.

I say she did—she loved me very well,
And I loved her until, ah, woe is me !
Until to-day, when passing through
    the dell
I met yourself, and now I cannot see
Her face at all, or any face but yours
In memory.

I ought to be ashamed ? well amn't I ?
But that's no comfort when I'm in a trap:
I tell you I shall sit down here and die
Unless you stay—you do not care a rap—
Ah, Little Sweetheart, do not run away,
. . . Have pity on a chap.

You'll go—then listen, you are just a pig,
A little wrinkled pig out of a sty ;
Your legs are crooked and your nose
    is big,
You've got no calves, you have a silly
    eye,
I don't know why I stopped to talk
    to you,
I hope you'll die.

Now cry, go on, mew like a little cat,
And rub your eyes and stamp and
    tear your wig ;
I see your ankles ! listen, they are fat,
And so's your head, you're angled like
    a twig,
Your back's all baggy and your clothes
    don't fit
And your feet are big !

She's gone, bedad, she legged it like a
    hare !
You'd think I had the itch, or had a
    face
Like a blue monkey—keeps me stand-
    ing there,
Not good enough to touch her . . . !
    Back I'll race
And make it up with Breed, that's
    what I'll do,
. . . *There is a flower that bloometh,*
Tra la la la laddy la. . . .

DANNY MURPHY

He was as old as old could be,
His little eye could scarcely see,
His mouth was sunken in between
His nose and chin, and he was lean
And twisted up and withered quite,
So that he could not walk aright.

His pipe was always going out,
And then he'd have to search about
In all his pockets, and he'd mow
—O, deary me ! and, musha now !
And then he'd light his pipe, and then
He'd let it go clean out again.

He could not dance or jump or run,
Or ever have a bit of fun

Like me and Susan, when we shout
And jump and throw ourselves about :
But when he laughed then you could
    see
He was as young as young could be.

THE TREE OF THE BIRD

I SAT beneath a tree
In a wide park,
There was a lark,
A bard of ecstasy,
Who sang amid the leaves of his beloved:
—" Thou art most fair,
None can with thee compare,"
Such was his minstrelsy.
" Thy flight is with the stars and with
    the wind,
And thou art kind,
O, my most well-beloved,"
And thus, and thus sang he.

The evening sun fell slowly to a hill
Far off and blue,

But I was too enraptured with the skill
Of that young songster, and the still
Slow rustle of the boughs
To heed how far the sun had stepped
Unto his western house.

A languor came upon me, sad
As was the peace that Adam had
When, on that woeful morning, he
Awaked to unknown misery,
And, all amazed, gave thanks to God
For the green tree, and the green sod,
For the clean wind, and for Eve's eyes,
For all that he had fancied lost
Of Paradise.

He did a moment furthermore
Outpour his many-patterned song,
Down to the ground,
Up to the sky,
About, around,
An ecstasy,
A sheer and sweet swift rush along;

And then the song failed, and he
    threw
His wings upon the air, and flew
Because he could no longer bide
From her whom he would nest beside.

A wind came breathing out of space
Blowing softly on my face;
The greying evening stept and stole
About the tree, till branch and bole
Were lost, and there remained to me
A rustling in a mystery:
And this—
A bliss, a happiness,
A song that had been a caress,
A memory of joy—which you,
And every one is welcome to.

PEADAR ÓG GOES COURTING

Now that I am dressed I'll go
Down to where the roses blow,
I'll pluck a fair and fragrant one
And make my mother pin it on :
Now she's laughing, so am I—
O the blueness of the sky !

Down the street, turn to the right,
Round the corner out of sight,
Pass the church and out of town—
Dust does show on boots of brown,
I'd better brush them while I can
—Step out, Peadar, be a man !

Here's a field and there's a stile,
Shall I jump it ? wait a while,
Scale it gently, stretch my foot
Across the mud in that big rut

And I'm still clean—faith, I'm not !
Get some grass and rub the spot.

Dodge those nettles, here the stream
Bubbles onward with a gleam
Steely white, and black, and grey,
Bending rushes on its way—
What's that moving ?   It's a rat
Washing his whiskers, isn't he fat ?

Here the cow with the crumpledy horn
Whisks her tail and looks forlorn,
She wants a milkmaid bad I guess
How her udders swell and press
Against her legs—and here's some sheep,
And there's the shepherd fast asleep.

This is a sad and lonely field,
Thistles are all that it can yield,
I'll cross it quick, nor look behind,
There's nothing in it but the wind :
And if those bandy-legged trees
Could talk they'd only curse or sneeze.

A sour, unhappy, sloppy place—
That boot's loose !   I'll tie the lace
So, and jump this little ditch,
. . . *Her father's really very rich* :
He'll be angry—there's a crow,
Solemn blackhead ! off you go.

There a big, grey, ancient ass
Is snoozing quiet in the grass,
He hears me coming, starts to rise,
Wags his big ears at the flies.
. . . *What'll I say when*—there's a frog,
Go it, long-legs, jig, jig-jog.

He'll be angry, say—" Pooh, pooh,
Boy, you know not what you do."
Shakespeare rot and good advice,
Fat old duffer—those field mice
Have a good time playing round
Through the corn and underground.

But her mother is friends with mine,
She always asks us out to dine,

And dear Nora, curly head,
Loves me ; so at least she said.
. . . Damn that ass's hee-hee-haw—
Was that a rabbit's tail I saw ?

This is the house, Lord, I'm afraid !
A man does suffer for a maid.
. . . *How will I start ?*—the graining's
 new
On the door—O pluck up, do.
Don't stand shivering there like that
. . . The knocker's funny—*rat-tat-tat.*

NORA CRIONA

I HAVE looked him round and looked
    him through,
Know everything that he will do
In such a case, and such a case,
And when a frown comes on his face
I dream of it, and when a smile
I trace its sources in a while.

He cannot do a thing but I
Peep to find the reason why,
For I love him, and I seek,
Every evening in the week,
To peep behind his frowning eye
With little query, little pry,
And make him if a woman can
Happier than any man.

Yesterday he gripped her tight
And cut her throat—and serve her right!

THE RUNE

The sun and the star,
The moon and the sea,
As they wandered afar
Sent a message to me.

For our friend, lovingly
We have fashioned a moral,
When there's room to agree
There is no room to quarrel.

And, therefore, we now
Send this thought to the friend
Whom we love, showing how
Every quarrel will end.

To be far brings you near,
But too near is too far ;
Can you love without fear
When the door's on the jar ?

BESSIE BOBTAIL

As down the street she wambled slow,
She had not got a place to go :
She had not got a place to fall
And rest herself—no place at all.
She stumped along and wagged her
    pate
And said a thing was desperate.

Her face was screwed and wrinkled
    tight
Just like a nut—and, left and right,
On either side she wagged her head
And said a thing, and what she said
Was desperate as any word
That ever yet a person heard.

I walked behind her for a while
And watched the people nudge and
    smile :
But ever as she went she said,
As left and right she swung her head,
—" *O God He knows,*" *and* " *God He*
    knows,
And, surely God Almighty knows."

THE TINKER'S BRAT

I saw a beggar woman bare
Her bosom to the winter air ;
And within the tender nest
Of her famished mother-breast
She laid her child,
And him beguiled,
With crooning song into his rest.

With crooning song and tender word,
About a little singing bird,
Who spread her wings about her
    brood,
And tore her bosom up for food,
And sang the while,
Them to beguile,
All in the forest's solitude.

And, hearing this, I could not see
That she was clad in misery ;
For in her heart there was a glow
Warmed her bare feet in the snow :
In her heart was hid a sun
Would warm a world for every one.

NOTHING AT ALL

THERE was a man was very old :
He sat beside a little fire,
And watched the flame begin to tire.

He held his hands out to the heat,
And in a voice was half a scold,
He told Creation he was cold.

And he was tired and feeble, too :
He could not lift up from his seat
To reach the fuel at his feet.

" Perhaps," said he, " God does not
    know
That I am nearly frozen through ;
He might not like it if He knew.

*   *   *   *   *

Poor old chattering, grumbling wight !
God will hardly come to fetch
Wood for such an ancient wretch.

But He will send you rain more cold,
To quench that little flickering light,
Like this, and He will freeze you quite :
. . . Men must die when they are old.

WHY TOMÁS CAM WAS GRUMPY

IF I were rich what would I do ?
I'd leave the horse just ready to
  shoe,
I'd leave the pail beside the cow,
I'd leave the furrow beneath the
  plough,
I'd leave the ducks tho' they should
  quack,
" Our eggs will be stolen before you're
  back " ;
I'd buy a diamond brooch, a ring,
A chain of gold that I would fling
Around her neck. . . . Ah, what an
  itch,
If I were rich !

What would I do if I were wise ?
I would not debate about the skies,
Nor would I try a book to write,
Or find the wrong in the tangled right,
I would not debate with learned men
Of how, and what, and why, and when ;
I'd train my tongue to a linnet's song,
I'd learn the words that couldn't go
　　wrong—
And then I'd say . . . And win the
　　prize,
If I were wise !

But I'm not that nor t'other, I bow
My back to the work that's waiting
　　now.
I'll shoe the horse that's standing
　　ready,
I'll milk the cow if she'll be steady,
I'll follow the plough that turns the
　　loam,
I'll watch the ducks don't lay from
　　home.

—And I'll curse, and curse, and curse
    again
Till the devil joins in with his big amen,
And none but he and I will wot
When the heart within me starts to rot,
To fester and churn its ugly brew—
, ₒ . Where's my spade ? I've work
    to do.

THE GIRL I LEFT BEHIND ME

SHE watched the blaze,
And so I said the thing I'd come to say,
Pondered for days.

Her lips moved slow,
And the wide eye she flashed on me
Was sudden as a blow.

She turned again,
Her hands clasping her knees and did
      not speak :
She did not deign.

And I, poor gnome !
A chided cur crawls to a hole to hide :
. . . I toddled home.

SHAME

I was ashamed, I dared not lift my
    eyes,
I could not bear to look upon the
    skies ;
What I had done ! sure, everybody
    knew !
From everywhere hands pointed where
    I stood,
And scornful eyes were piercing through
    and through
The moody armour of my hardihood.

I heard their voices too, each word an
    asp
That buzz'd and stung me sudden as
    a flame :

And all the world was jolting on my
    name,
And now and then there came a
    wicked rasp
Of laughter, jarring me to deeper
    shame.

And then I looked, but there was no
    one nigh,
No eyes that stabbed like swords or
    glinted sly,
No laughter creaking on the silent air :
And then I found that I was all alone
Facing my soul, and next I was aware
That this mad mockery was all my
    own.

I WISH

I wish I had not grown to man's
    estate,
I wish I was a silly urchin still,
With bounding pulses and a heart elate
To meet whatever came of good or ill.

Of good or ill ! not knowing what was
    good,
But groping to a better than I knew,
And guessing deeper than I under-
    stood,
And hoping truths that never could be
    true.

Of good or ill ! when, so it often seems,
There is no good at all but only ill.

72

Alas, the sunny summer - time of
    dreams,
The dragons I had nerved my hand to
    kill,
The maids I might have rescued, and
    the queen
Whose champion long ago I could
    have been.

SECRETS

When I was young I used to think,
That every eye peered through a chink,
And every man was hid behind
His own thick self where none could
    find.

That every woman in the street,
Looking fair and smiling sweet,
Was maybe hiding thoughts that were
Not quite so sweet, nor quite so fair
As her kind smile and blossom face ;
She hid in some forgotten place
Within herself and would not dare
To let another see her there.

And though I'm older still I see
In every face a mystery.

CROOKED-HEART

I LOOSED an arrow from my bow
Down into the world below;
Thinking " This will surely dart,
Guided by my guiding fate,
Into the malignant heart
Of the person whom I hate."

So by hatred feathered well
Swift the flashing arrow fell:
And I watched it from above
Disappear
Cleaving sheer
Through the only heart I love.

Such the guard my angels keep!
But my foe is guarded well:
I have slain my love and weep
Tears of blood, while he, asleep,
Does not know an arrow fell!

MAC DHOUL

I saw them all,
I could have laughed out loud
To see them at their capers ;
That serious, solemn-footed, weighty
    crowd
Of angels, or say resurrected drapers :
Each with a thin flame swinging round
    his head,
With lilting wings and eyes of holy
    dread,
And curving ears strained for the great
    foot-fall,
And not a thought of sin— . . .
I don't know how I kept the laughter
    in.

For I was there,
Unknown, unguessed at, snug
In a rose tree's branchy spurt,
With two weeks' whisker blackening
    lug to lug,
With tattered breeks and only half a
    shirt.
Swollen fit to burst with laughter at
    the sight
Of those dull angels drooping left and
    right
Along the towering throne, each in a
    scare
To hear His foot advance
Huge from the cloud behind, all in a
    trance.

And suddenly,
As silent as a ghost,
I jumped out from the bush,
Went scooting through the glaring,
    nerveless host
All petrified, all gaping in a hush :

Came to the throne and, nimble as a rat,
Hopped up it, squatted close, and
    there I sat,
Squirming with laughter till I had to cry,
To see Him standing there
Frozen with all His angels in a stare !

He raised His hand,
His hand ! 'twas like a sky !
Gripped me in half a finger,
Flipped me round and sent me spin-
    ning high
Through screaming planets : faith, I
    didn't linger
To scratch myself, and then adown I
    sped
Scraping old moons and twisting heels
    and head,
A chuckle in the void, till . . . here I
    stand
As naked as a brick,
I'll sing the Peeler and the Goat in
    half a tick.

THE MERRY POLICEMAN

I was appointed guardian by
The Power that frowns along the sky,
To watch the tree and see that none
Plucked of the fruit that grew thereon.

There was a robber in the tree,
Who climbed as high as ever he
Was able, at the top he knew
The apple of all apples grew.

The night was dark, the branch was
    thin,
In every wind he heard the din
Of angels calling—" Guardian, see
That no one climbs upon the tree."

And when he saw me standing there
He shook with terror and despair,
But I said to him—" Be at rest,
The best to him who wants the best."

So I was sacked, but I have got
A job in hell to keep me hot.

THE FAIRY BOY

A LITTLE Fairy in a tree
Wrinkled his wee face at me :
And he sang a song of joy
All about a little boy,
Who upon a winter night,
On a midnight long ago,
Had been wrapt away from sight
Of the world and all its woe :
Wrapt away,
Snapt away
To a place where children play
In the sunlight every day.

Where the winter is forbidden,
Where no child may older grow,
Where a flower is never hidden
Underneath a pall of snow ;

Dancing gaily
Free from sorrow,
Under dancing summer skies,
Where no grim mysterious morrow
Ever comes to terrorize.

This I told a priest and he
Spoke a word of mystery,
And with candle, book and bell,
Tolling Latin like a knell,
Ruthlessly
From the tree,
Sprinkling holy water round,
He drove the Fairy down to hell,
There in torment to be bound.

So the tree is withered and
There is sorrow on the land :
But the devils milder grow
Dancing gay
Every day
In that kinder land below :
There the devils dance for joy
And love that little wrinkled boy.

WHAT THE DEVIL SAID

IT was the night time, God the Father
    Good,
Weary of praises, on a sudden stood
Up from His throne and leaned upon
    the sky,
For He had heard a sound, a little
    cry,
Thin as a whisper climbing up the
    steep.

And He looked down to where the
    Earth asleep
Rocked with the moon, He saw the
    whirling sea
Swing round the world in surgent
    energy,

Tangling the moonlight in its netted
        foam,
And nearer saw the white and fretted
        dome
Of the ice-capped pole spin back again
        a ray
To whistling stars, bright as a wizard's
        day.

But these He passed with eyes intently
        wide,
Till closer still the mountains He espied
Squatting tremendous on the broad-
        backed Earth ;
Each nursing twenty rivers at a birth.
And then minutely sought He for the
        cry
Had climbed the slant of space so
        hugely high.

He found it in a ditch outside a town,
A tattered, hungry woman crouching
        down

By a dead babe—so there was nought
    to do,
For what is done is done; and back
    He drew
Sad to His Heaven of ivory and gold;
And as He sat, all suddenly there rolled
From where the woman wept upon the
    sod
Satan's deep voice, " *O thou unhappy*
    God ! "

TO THE TREE

BALLAD ! I have a message you must
    bear
Unto a certain tree : I may not tell
Where she abides, only, she is more fair
Than any tree that grows down in a
    dell,
Or on a mountain top, or by a well,
Or as a lovely sentinel beside
A roaming stream. No words can
    speak her well,
Nor lyric sing enough her arms so wide,
Her grace, her peace, her innocence,
    her happy pride.

Come, Ballad, quickly back to me
    again,

After you have delivered to the tree
My humble service, and if she will deign
To trust you with a message back,
    then see
You strictly do forget no word that she
May speak to you, no smallest yes or no:
And what she looked like when she
    spoke of me,
And if she begged you stay or bade
    you go,
Or hesitated ere she said—what you
    shall know.

Say—I shall be with her ere day is
    done,
When the flushed evening blanches to
    the dark,
And one last gleam of all that was the
    sun
Rests on her topmost branches, when
    the lark
Dips to the dew-steeped grasses in the
    park

And only now and then sends from
    below
A sleepy song : then, swift as to the
    mark
An arrow flies, so swiftly will I go
Nor stay until her branches wide I
    halt below.

There is a crow, of sly and wicked
    fame,
Whom, with Apollo's aid, I hope to slay,
For he has dared and come nigh to
    my dame
And in her heart would hide him well
    away :
A wicked crow is he and hoary-grey ;
He listens to the life that throbs so
    fleet
Along the trunk and by the slender way
Of her young veins whereat the
    branches meet :
A curious, bad, old, wicked crow and
    indiscreet.

Of every tree most beautiful and
    queen !
The grasses at her feet live in her glee,
About her all the forest folk are seen ;
The timid nymph bends there a ready
    knee,
And mighty Pan himself, unwillingly,
Yet all perforce, must stoop before
    her grace,
And round about in a wild ecstasy
The light-foot satyrs (stayed from an
    embrace)
Stare shamefully and dance and mince
    with antic pace.

Fortress of melody ! Well hidden
    heart !
Deep bosomed lady whom I love so well !
Dear solitude of singer without art !
Sweet shadiness wherein I long to
    dwell,
Enrapt and comforted from any spell
Of thought or care or woefulness or sin ;

Or trouble which a man may not fore-
    tell ;
Or slothful ease which it is death to win;
Or fear that cometh at the last and
    creepeth in.

If you among her little leaves will fly
And what they whisper bring to me
    again,
Dear Ballad, I will write your history
Upon a sheepskin with a golden pen ;
It shall be read by women and by men :
Each youth will sing it to his paramour
As they go roving in the evening when
All joy is innocence and love is lore,
And you and youth and love will live
    for evermore.

Rapture and joy and ecstasy and pain !
The windy trumpets of the void shall
    soar
Over the sky. The Morning Stars
    again

Will sing together joyous as of yore :
The sea shall tramp with banners on
 the shore :
The little hills skip merrily along
The forest leave its field and with a
 roar
Stride down the pathway shouting out
 a song,
And everything be happy as the day
 is long.

Envoi

Ballad, farewell ! go tell her that I
 burn,
Say that I die if she refuses me :
And I shall wait and sigh till you
 return,
And plague the god of life and love
 to favour me.

ORA PRO NOBIS

A BIRD sings now;
Merrily
Sings he
Of his mate on the bough,
And her eggs in the tree;
But yonder a hawk
Swoops out of the blue
And the singing is over
—Is this true?
God now have mercy on me and on
you.

THE END OF THE ROAD

To Æ.

THIS is a thing is true,
Everything comes to an end :
The loving of me and you,
The walking of friend and friend.

Shall I weep the beauty I knew,
Or the greatness gathered away
Or the truth that is only true,
As the things that a man will say ?

The child and the mother will die,
The wife and husband sever,
The sun will go out of the sky,
And the rain will be falling for ever.

For ever until the waves rear
To the skies with a terrible tune,
And cover the earth and the air,
And wash up the beach of the moon.

Then go, for all things must end,
And this is true as I say—
A friend will be leaving a friend,
And a man will be going away.

WIND AND TREE

To Æ.

" A WOMAN is a branchy tree
  And man a singing wind,
  And from her branches carelessly
  He takes what he can find :
  Then wind and man go far away
  While winter comes with loneliness,
  With cold and rain and slow decay
  On woman and on tree till they
  Droop to the ground again and be
  A withered woman, a withered tree ;
  While wind and man woo undismayed
  Another tree, another maid."

EVE

Long ago, in ages grey,
I was fashioned out of clay :
Builded with the sun and moon,
Kneaded to a holy tune ;
And there came to me a breath
From the House of Life and Death.

Then the sun roared into fire,
And the moon with swift desire
Leaped among the starry throng
Singing on her journey long ;
And I climbed up from the sod,
Holding to the hand of God.

In a garden fair and wide
Looking down a mountain side,
Prone I lay and felt the press
Of Immensity's caress,

There I lived a space and knew
What the Power meant to do.

Till upon a day there came
Down to me a voice of flame,
" Thou the corner-stone of man,
Rise and set about my plan,
Nothing doubting, for a guide
I have quickened in thy side."

From the garden wide and fair,
From the pure and holy air,
Down the mountain side I crept
Stumbling often, ill-adept ;
Feeling pangs of woeful bliss,
Rounding from the primal kiss.

Then from out my straining side
Came the son who is my guide :
Him I nursed through faithful days
Till I faltered at his gaze,
Staring boldly when he saw
I was woman, life, and law.

H

Life and law and dear delight :
I the moon upon the night
All alluring : I the tree
Growing nuts of mystery :
I the tincture and the dew
That the apple reddens through.

Weaving Life and Death I go :
Building what I do not know :
Planting tho' in sore distress,
Gardens in the wilderness :
Palaces too big to scan
By the little eye of man.

Still the sun roars out in fire,
And the moon with pale desire
Keeps the path appointed her
In the starry theatre :
Sun and moon and I are true,
To the work we have to do.

THE BREATH OF LIFE

(*To Elizabeth Bloxham*)

AND while they talked and talked, and
while they sat
Changing their base minds into baser
coin ;
And telling—they ! how truth and
beauty join,
And how a certain this was good, but
that
Was baser than the viper or the toad,
Or the blind beggar glaring down the
road.

I turned from them in fury, and I ran
To where the moon shone out upon
the height,

Down the long reaches of a summer
    night
Stretching slim fingers, and the starry
    clan
Grew thicker than the flowers that we
    see
Clustered in quiet fields of greenery.

The quietudes that sunder star from
    star,
The hazy distances of loneliness,
Where never eagle's wing or timid press
Of lark or wren could venture, and the
    far
Profundities untravelled and unstirred
By any act of man or thought or word.

These held me with amazement and
    delight :
I yearned up through the spaces of
    the sky,
Beyond the rolling clouds, beyond the
    high

And delicate white moon, and up the
    height,
And past the rocking stars, and out to
    where
The aether failed in spaces sharp and
    bare.

The breath that is the very breath of
    life
Throbbed close to me : I heard the
    pulses beat,
That lift the universes into heat :
The slow withdrawal, and the deeper
    strife
Of His wide respiration, like a sea
It ebbed and flooded through im-
    mensity.

The Breath of Life in wave on mighty
    wave !
O moon and stars swell to a raptured
    song !
Ye mountains toss the harmony along !

O little men with little souls to save
Swing up glad chantings, ring the
    skies above,
With boundless gratitude for bound-
    less love !

Probing the ocean to its steepest drop ;
Rejoicing in the viper and the toad,
And the blind beggar glaring down the
    road ;
And they who talk and talk and never
    stop
Equally quickening ; with a care to
    bend
The gnat's slant wing into a swifter
    end.

*   *   *   *   *

The silence clung about me like a gift,
The tender night-time folded me around
Protectingly, and in a peace profound
The clouds drooped slowly backward,
    drift on drift

Into the darkness, and the moon was
    gone,
And soon the stars had vanished every
    one.

But on the sky, a handsbreadth in the
    west,
A faint cold radiance crept and soared
    and spread,
Until the rustling heavens overhead,
And the grey trees and grass were
    manifest :
Then through the chill a golden spear
    was hurled,
And the great sun tossed laughter on
    the world.

IN THE COOL OF THE EVENING

I THOUGHT I heard Him calling! Did
  you hear
A sound, a little sound? My curious
  ear
Is dinned with flying noises, and the
  tree
Goes — whisper, whisper, whisper
  silently,
Till all its whispers spread into the
  sound
Of a dull roar . . . Lie closer to the
  ground,
The shade is deep and He may pass
  us by,
We are so very small, and His great
  eye,

Customed to starry majesties, may
    gaze
Too wide to spy us hiding in the maze :
—Ah, misery ! the sun has not yet gone
And we are naked : He will look upon
Our crouching shame, may make us
    stand upright
Burning in terror—O that it were
    night !
He may not come . . . What ? listen,
    listen, now—
He's here ! lie closer . . . *Adam, where
    art thou ?*

PSYCHOMETRIST

I LISTENED to a man and he
Had no word to say to me :
Then unto a stone I bowed,
And it spoke to me aloud.

" The force that bindeth me so long,
Once sang in the linnet's song,
Now upon the ground I lie,
While the centuries go by.

" Linnets must for joy atone
And be fastened into stone,
While upon the waving tree
Stones shall sing in energy."

THE WINGED TRAMP

I SAW a poor man walking slow,
Scarcely knowing where to go ;
And from door to door he said,
Unto those who stood within,
—" Give me, with a little bread,
Absolution for my sin."

And the people always said,
—" Friend, come in and eat our bread ;
Lay you down and rest a while,
Sleep a little time and pray
Unto God and He will smile
All your weighty sin away."

Then the poor man rose and flew
In the air, and no one knew

That He was God's beloved Son :
And He told His Father plain
What the folk had said and done :
—So God spared the world again.

THE MONKEY'S COUSIN

I SHALL reach up, I shall grow
Till the high gods say—" Hello,
Little brother, you must stop
Ere our shoulders you o'ertop."

I shall grow up, I shall reach
Till the little gods beseech
—" Master, wait a little, do,
We are running after you ! "

I shall bulk and swell and scale
Till the little gods shall quail,
Running here and there to hide
From the terror of my stride.

THE LONELY GOD

(*To Stephen MacKenna*)

So Eden was deserted, and at eve
Into the quiet place God came to
grieve.
His face was sad, His hands hung
slackly down
Along His robe, too sorrowful to frown
He paced along the grassy paths and
through
The silent trees, and where sweet
flowers grew
Tended by Adam. All the birds had
gone
Out to the world, and there was left
not one
To sing the lonely God out of His
grief—

The silence broken only when a leaf
Tapt lightly on a leaf, or when the
     wind,
Slow-handed, swayed the bushes to its
     mind.

And so along the base of a round hill,
Rolling in fern, He bent His way
     until
He neared the little hut which Adam
     made,
And saw its dusky roof-tree overlaid
With greenest leaves.   Here Adam and
     his spouse
Were wont to nestle in their little house
Snug at the dew-time : here He, stand-
     ing sad,
Sighed with the wind, nor any pleasure
     had
In heavenly knowledge, for His dar-
     lings twain,
Had gone from Him to learn the mode
     of pain,

And what was meant by sorrow and
    despair,
—Drear knowledge for a Father to
    prepare.

There He looked sadly on the little
    place,
A beehive round it was, without a trace
Of occupant or owner : standing dim
Among the gloomy trees it seemed to
    Him
A final desolation, the last word
Wherewith the lips of silence had been
    stirred.
Chaste and remote, so tiny and so
    shy,
So new withal, so lost to any eye,
So pac't of memories all innocent
Of days and nights that in it had been
    spent
In blithe communion, Adam, Eve, and
    He,
Afar from Heaven and its gaudery.

And now no more ! He still must be
    the God
But not the friend; a Father with a
    rod
Whose voice was fear, whose counte-
    nance a threat,
Whose coming terror, and whose going
    wet
With penitential tears ; not evermore
Would they run forth to meet Him as
    before
With careless laughter, striving each
    to be
First to His hand and dancing in their
    glee
To see Him coming—They would hide
    instead
At His approach, or stand and hang
    the head,
Speaking in whispers, and would learn
    to pray
Instead of asking, "Father. if we
    may."

I

Never again to Eden would He haste
At cool of evening, when the sun had
    paced
Back from the tree-tops, slanting from
    the rim
Of a low cloud, what time the twilight
    dim,
Knit tree to tree in shadow, gathering
    slow
Till all had met and vanished in the
    flow
Of dusky silence, and a brooding star
Stared at the growing darkness from
    afar,
While haply now and then some nested
    bird
Would lift upon the air a sleepy word
Most musical, or swing its airy bed
To the high moon that drifted over-
    head.

'Twas good to quit at evening His
    great throne,

To lay His crown aside, and all alone
To stoop down quiet airs at eventide
Unkenned by angels : silently to hide
In the green fields, by dappled shades,
    where brooks,
Through leafy solitudes and quiet
    nooks
Flowed far from heavenly majesty and
    pride,
From light astounding and the wheel-
    ing tide
Of roaring stars. Thus does it ever
    seem
Good to the best to stay aside and
    dream
In narrow places, where the hand can
    feel
Something beside, and know that it is
    real.

His angels !   Silly creatures who could
    sing
And sing again, and delicately fling

The smoky censer, bow and stand
     aside
All mute in adoration : thronging
     wide,
Till nowhere could He look but soon
     He saw
An angel bending humbly to the
     law
Mechanic ; knowing nothing more of
     pain,
Than when they were forbid to sing
     again,
Or swing anew the censer, or bow
     down,
In humble adoration of His frown.
This was the thought in Eden as He
     trod
. . . It is a lonely thing to be a God.

So long !   Afar through Time He bent
     His mind,
For the beginning, which He could
     not find,

Through endless centuries and back-
    wards still
Endless for ever, till His 'stonied will
Halted in circles, dizzied in the swing
Of mazy nothingness—His mind could
    bring
Not to subjection, grip or hold the
    theme
Whose wide horizon melted like a dream
To thinnest edges.   Infinite behind
The piling centuries were trodden
    blind
In gulfs chaotic—so He could not see
When He was not who always had
    To Be.

O solitude unspeakable ! to be
For ever with oneself ! never to see
An equal face, or feel an equal hand,
To sit in state and issue reprimand,
Admonishment or glory, and to smile
Disdaining what has happened the
    while !

O to be breast to breast against a foe !
Against a friend ! to strive and not
    to know
The laboured outcome : Love nor be
    aware
How much the other loved, and greatly
    care
With passion for that happy love or
    hate,
Nor know what joy or dole was hid
    in fate.

" For I have ranged the spacy width
    and gone
Swift north and south, striving to
    look upon
An ending somewhere.   Many days I
    sped
Hard to the west, a thousand years I
    fled
Eastwards in fury, but I could not
    find
The fringes of the Infinite.   Behind

And yet behind, and ever at the end
Came new beginnings, paths that did
    not wend
To anywhere were there: and ever vast
And vaster spaces opened—till at last
Dizzied with distance, thrilling to a
    pain
Unnameable, I turned to Heaven again.

" And there My angels were prepared
    to fling
The cloudy incense, there prepared to
    sing
My praise and glory—O, in fury I
Then roared them senseless, then threw
    down the sky
And stamped upon it, buffeted a star
With My great fist, and flung the sun
    afar :
Shouted My anger till the mighty
    sound
Rung to the width, frighting the
    furthest bound

And scope of hearing : tumult vaster
    still,
Thronging the echo, dinned my ears,
    until
I fled in silence, seeking out a place
To hide Me from the very thought of
    Space.

"And so," He thought, "in Mine own
    Image I
Have made a man, remote from
    Heaven high
And all its humble angels : I have
    poured
My essence in his nostrils : I have
    cored
His heart with My own spirit ; part
    of Me
His mind with laboured growth un-
    ceasingly
Must strive to equal Mine ; must ever
    grow
By virtue of My essence till he know

Both good and evil through the solemn
    test
Of sin and retribution, till, with zest,
He feels his godhead, soars to challenge
    Me
In Mine own Heaven for supremacy.

"Through savage beasts and still more
    savage clay,
Invincible, I bid him fight a way
To greater battles, crawling through
    defeat
Into defeat again : ordained to meet
Disaster in disaster : prone to fall
I prick him with My memory to call
Defiance at his victor and arise
With anguished fury to his greater
    size
Through tribulation, terror and despair
Astounded, he must fight to higher air,
Climb battle into battle till he be
Confronted with a flaming sword and
    Me.

" The topmost blossom of his growing I
Shall take unto Me, cherish and lift high
Beside Myself upon My holy throne :
—It is not good for God to be alone.
The perfect woman of his perfect race
Shall sit beside Me in the highest place
And be My Goddess, Queen, Com-
    panion, Wife,
The rounder of My majesty, the life,
Of My ambition.   She will smile to see
Me bending down in worship at her
    knee
Who never bent before, and she will
    say,
—" Dear God, who was it taught *Thee*
    how to pray ? "

"And through eternity, adown the
    slope
Of never-ending time, compact of hope,
Of zest and young enjoyment, I and
    She
Will walk together, sowing jollity

Among the raving stars, and laughter
    through
The vacancies of Heaven, till the blue
Vast amplitudes of space lift up a song,
The echo of our presence, rolled along
And ever rolling where the planets sing
The majesty and glory of the King.
Then conquered, thou, eternity, shall
    lie
Under my hand as little as a fly."

Then stooping to the hut—a beehive
    round—
God entered in and saw upon the
    ground
The dusty garland, Adam, (learned to
    weave)
Had loving placed upon the head of
    Eve
Before the terror came, when joyous
    they
Could look for God at closing of the
    day

Profound and happy.   So the Mighty
    Guest
Bent, took, and placed the blossoms
    in His breast.
" This," said He gently, " I shall show
    My queen
When she hath grown to Me in space
    serene,
And say ' 'twas worn by Eve.' "   So,
    smiling fair,
He spread abroad His wings upon the
    air.

THE END

Printed in Great Britain by R. & R. Clark, Limited, *Edinburgh.*